Authors
Colette Stone and Elizabeth Stone
Illustrator – Zoe Laverne
Editor – John Hansen

Copyrigt2021

Dedicated Page

To every child: accept yourself and others

This Book Belongs To:

_____

_____

How do you do? My name is Jamie,
When you look at me, what can you see?
My short curly red hair and big eyes of blue,
My knobbly knees, or the things that I do?

Maybe it's my glasses in a bright shade of green,
The coolest glasses that you've ever seen,
Or because I am tall and thin like the trees?
No, you must be looking at my knobbly knees.

This is my mum, she is a star,
I like to watch when she is fixing the car.
We both like to jump up and down in puddles,
And she always gives me plenty of cuddles.

We always sit down and talk every day
But mum always worries when I go out to play.
I am allowed outside within her eyesight,
To play and have fun but be inside by night.

Where is my dad? Is he hiding again?
Slouching in his favourite chair, snoozing for ten,
Or in the garage secretly drinking beer?
Though he stops doing that if ever I'm near.

He may be near the cookie jar, or eating some jelly?
No wonder he has such a great big belly.
Dad works hard at his job, but relaxes at home,
He spends his time sleeping or checking his phone.

Here is my Grandpa Joe and Grandma Nelly,
They are much older than me and never watch telly.
Grandma Nelly loves to dance,
round and round we both go,
Whilst Grandpa Joe plays badly on his piano.

Grandma and Grandpa both like to have fun,
They tell funny stories of what they have done.
They rarely get upset and often joke around,
I'm sure Grandpa Joe once was a clown.

My family are all different, like elephants and giraffes,
But they are all warm and caring and make me laugh.
My family listen to me when I have concerns,
They give me advice but are willing to learn.

At school I'm a loner, I don't have any friends.
I don't know the reason, I guess that depends.
I like my teachers and enjoy my classes,
Maybe it's because I have red hair and glasses?

My parents tell me, "Try not to be sad,
We are proud to be your Mum and your Dad.
You will make friends who accept you however you are,
Just be yourself Jamie, because you're a star".

I stand in the playground, sad, all by myself,
seeing children who look different, like books on a shelf.
Everyone is playing, skipping, and running so fast,
They are all smiling and laughing and having a blast.

If they all look different maybe I'll fit in too,
I'll try to join in and stop feeling blue.
They are all very kind and now we are friends,
I hope all the fun we have just never ends.

My family were pleased with the new friends I had made,
They said I seemed happier, and they welcomed the change.
Mum said, "We must meet them, ask your friends around to play.
And if they're allowed, for tea they can stay."

I invited my new friends home to share tea,
One at a time with just my family and me.
But my family all act different than I thought they would.
They behave as though my friends are not good.

Mum told me to invite them, it was her idea.
So I don't understand why they don't want them here.
My friends are polite, and neither are rude,
They even complimented Dad's food.

My Dad really seems uncomfortable with Tim
I do not understand Dad's problem with him.
I see how he goes quiet and turns the other way,
Even when Tim tries to speak to him every day.

One day Tim and I were competing in a race,
But Dad kept looking at my friend's face.
"Tim's nose is different from yours," says my dad.
His eyes are different too," and he looked a bit sad.

Why does Grandpa Joe make that weird face?
Is it because I fell over, and Tim won the race?
And Grandma Nelly has the very same look
I know she is pretending to be reading that book.

And why doesn't my Mum like my friend Sue?
She said, "Jamie, your friend looks different than you,
Her hair and her skin are a darker colour.
Where do they come from, her father and mother?"

There is something that is troubling my mind.
My family said to always be polite and kind.
Be friendly to everyone and always share.
So, why don't they accept my friends? That's not fair.

I'm sure they aren't happy with the new friends I made,
Why do they think we should all look the same?
It is how people treat you that makes them a friend,
Nothing else really matters in the end.

I love Mum and Dad, Grandma, Grandpa too,
I appreciate everything each of them do.
But my friends are important I had to explain,
And I'd choose the same ones if I had to again.

So, I gathered my family and told them my thoughts
I repeated the values I'd always been taught.
Be kind and accepting, don't judge, always share,
Choose friends who don't bully but show that they care.

What people look like does not really matter,
Taller, shorter, skinnier, or fatter.
Dark skin or light skin, blue eyes or brown.
Smile at each other, there's no need to frown.

Apart from our family name,
None of us are the same.
We each have different eyes, hair, mouths, and skin,
But none of those matters, it's the bond that's within.

Dad, Mum's eyes are different from yours
Are you not her friend, and love her just because?
Mum, Dads' nose is different from yours
Are you not his friend, even though he snores?

Grandpa Joe, your skin is different from mine
Are we not friends, and get along fine?
Grandma Nelly, your hair is different from mine
Are we not friends, and always have a good time?

Mum, you're a writer, and Dad is a cook,
He makes great desserts, and you write great books.
I'm not sure yet, what I want to be,
But whatever I choose, you'll both support me.

You see my friends will always be different from me.
They like to skateboard, and I'd rather climb trees.
I like ketchup and Tim prefers mustard,
Sue likes cream, but I prefer custard.

My hair is curly, and Tim's hair is straight.
He's always early, and I'm always late.
Sue's eyes are brown and mine are blue.
My hair is red, and jet black is Sue's

Tim eats with chopsticks and I use knife and fork,
I am a bit quiet, but Sue loves to talk.
Sue is so smart, she's top of the class,
Tim and I are lucky if we just get a pass.

My friends support me, they share, and are kind.
They stop and wait if I fall behind.
We all take turns to do things we love,
We don't hurt each other, never push and shove.

So, please take the advice you gave me for free
Accept all my friends just like you do me.
They are all good children, and don't disrespect,
I don't know what else you really expect.

My friends are there for me, just like all of you.
They may not be family, but their friendship is true.
They are my best friends and will always be.
Just like we are family, and that's as it should be

Friendship and unity is what we should seek.
Accepting each other, and how we look and speak.
We shouldn't judge others,
because they aren't the same,
We all enjoy kindness and playing fun games.

The End

About the Author

Colette Stone and Elizabeth Stone combined their skills, experiences, and interests in the creation of a collection of children's books. Colette Stone is studying English, History and Philosophy. She has always had a deep interest in philosophy and politics, and she is looking to specialize in those domains with Law sprinkled in that mix. With a doctoral degree in Science, Elizabeth spent years in that field and even published a few papers before moving on to international marketing for a few years. This dynamic duo began their storytelling journey, verbally or written, right when Colette Stone was born.

After years of putting their creativity on the back burner, they finally took the leap of faith and decided to bring their stories to life through the children's eyes. The books are spread across a variety of topics, from fictional to early childhood education with a dash of humour. Colette and Elizabeth incorporate life lessons in their publications using their own journeys and the difficulties they faced as a multicultural family. The essence of this collection of books is to capture the memories - good and bad- they have had through life and inspire the children around the world. The pair aims to make reading and learning fun for children.

In that same spirit, they embarked on a new venture and launched 2 of Us Studio, a publishing company that focuses on children's books. Beyond inspiring children and people across the world, as creative women, they are always looking to be inspired by others. One of their strongest characteristics is they consistently take the time to sit down, listen and participate in each other's stories. As mother and daughter, Elizabeth, and Colette value family more than anything. They have a very close bond, and they never miss an opportunity to have a good laugh.

Printed in Great Britain
by Amazon

14945493R00025